How to Dazzle at

WRITTEN CALCULATIONS

Beryl Webber and Jean Haigh

Brilliant Publications

We hope you and your class enjoy using this book. Other books in the series include:

Maths titles
How to Dazzle at Algebra   1 903853 12 5
How to Dazzle at Oral and Mental Starters   1 903853 10 9

English titles
How to Dazzle at Writing   1 897675 45 3
How to Dazzle at Reading   1 897675 44 5
How to Dazzle at Spelling   1 897675 47 X
How to Dazzle at Grammar   1 897675 46 1
How to Dazzle at Reading for Meaning   1 897675 51 8

Science title
How to Dazzle at Being a Scientist   1 897675 52 6

ICT title
How to Dazzle at Information Technology   1 897675 67 4

If you would like further information on these or other titles published by Brilliant Publications, please write to the address given below.

Published by Brilliant Publications, 1 Church View, Sparrow Hall Farm, Edlesborough, Dunstable, Bedfordshire LU6 2ES

Telephone: 01525 229720
Fax: 01525 229725

email: sales@brilliantpublications.co.uk
website: www.brilliantpublications.co.uk

Written by Beryl Webber and Jean Haigh
Illustrated by Sue Woollatt of Graham Cameron Illustrations

Printed in Malta by Interprint Limited

© Beryl Webber and Jean Haigh 2002
ISBN 1 903853 11 7

First published 2002
10 9 8 7 6 5 4 3 2 1

Contents

Introduction

How to Dazzle at Written Calculations contains 43 photocopiable sheets for use with pupils aged 11 to 13 who are working at levels 2–3 of the National Curriculum. The activities are presented in an age-appropriate manner and provide a flexible but structured resource for teaching pupils to understand written methods for all four mathematical operations. The tasks are varied but repeat these operations in a range of contexts and using different approaches. Each task is linked to the National Numeracy Strategy Framework for Key Stage 3. The tasks can be introduced to pupils in mixed-ability classes or are suitable to be undertaken by pupils working in the lower sets in Years 7 and 8.

These pupils will have had many years working on these mathematical concepts during their primary school education and it is important to ensure that the fundamental principles of the number system are understood before embarking on the tasks. The tasks are intended to support direct teaching and give teachers some evidence to assess pupils' understanding of addition, subtraction, multiplication and division. Multiplication and division activities using a range of strategies are provided in order to give pupils opportunities to find a method that they understand and that works for them.

The sheets are designed to give pupils opportunities to succeed in their mathematics. The expectation that the pupil will experience success will help to build confidence and competence.

Most of the tasks are fairly short to facilitate concentration. The text is kept to a minimum. The language of the contextualized tasks is more complex due to the age-appropriateness of the context. Many of the tasks have an investigative element or are in the form of a shared activity so that pupils may work together, thus consolidating the mathematical vocabulary that is fundamental to the National Numeracy Strategy. The extra Add-on task at the end of most sheets provides reinforcement and challenge.

How to use the book

The activity sheets are designed to supplement any numeracy programme you undertake in the classroom. They are intended to add to the pupils' knowledge of the four rules of number and give opportunities to try different methods of working. There are also some contextualized activities that will require the pupils to discuss the operation(s) to apply to solve the problem.

The sheets can be used with individual pupils, pairs or very small groups, as the need arises. The mathematics is linked to the learning objectives for Year 7. Pupils with poor reading skills may need support with the problems. However, they should be able to extract the mathematics themselves and decide on the correct operation to apply. Some of the activities can be used during the main part of the lesson to enable a mixed-ability class to work on a similar theme. The pupils will then be able to interact during the plenary to share what they have been learning.

It is not the intention of the authors that the teacher should expect all the pupils to complete all the sheets, rather that the sheets be used with a flexible approach, so that the book will provide a bank of resources that will meet pupils' needs as they arise.

Many of the sheets can be modified and extended by creating further examples. The Add-ons provide a good vehicle for discussion of what has been learned and how it can be applied. The Add-ons should always be included in any class or group discussion at the end of the lesson or in some cases may be suitable as homework tasks for discussion at a later date. There is a product square on page 48 to be photocopied and given to each pupil to attach to his or her mathematics workbook or folder. Pupils should be encouraged to use the product square when they are unsure of their multiplication and division facts.

The two check tests on pages 46 and 47 use much of the vocabulary identified in the book and focus on the range of problems set out in the activity sheets. There are just ten questions in each test to give you enough time to work with pupils who are having difficulties reading the mathematical vocabulary. These tests can be used to identify the progress pupils have made in their understanding of mathematical vocabulary and written calculations.

Addition and subtraction words

Look at these words. Check you know what they mean.
Sort them into two groups. Which words are hardest to sort?
Why is that?

increase	add	**sum**
more than	less than	plus
total	take away	**decrease**
subtract	**difference**	minus
altogether		

+

−

Add-on
Make up sentences using the words in **bold**.

What's my addition?

My answer was 19.
Which 2 numbers did I add?

[　　] + [　　] = 19

My answer was 19.
Which 3 numbers did I add?

[　　] + [　　] + [　　] = 19

My answer was 19.
I started at 50.
Which 2 negative numbers did I add?

50 + [−] + [−] = 19

My answer was 19.
I started at 50.
Which 3 negative numbers did I add?

50 + [−] + [−] + [−] = 19

My answer was 19.
I added 1 negative number and 1 positive number.
What were my numbers?

[−] + [　　] = 19

My answer was 19.
I added 2 positive numbers and 1 negative number.
What were my numbers?

[　　] + [　　] + [−] = 19

My answer was 19.
I added 2 positive numbers and 2 negative numbers.
What were my numbers?

[　　] + [　　] + [−] + [−] = 19

Add-on
What would happen if the answer was changed to 20 or 18? What can you say about the solutions?

What's my subtraction?

My answer was 3.
Which 2 numbers did I use?

$$\boxed{} - \boxed{} = 3$$

Hint:
Each one has many correct solutions.
Use a number line to help you.

My answer was 3. I started with a positive number.
I subtracted a negative number.
What were my numbers?

$$\boxed{+} - \boxed{-} = 3$$

My answer was 3. I started with a positive number.
I subtracted a positive number and a negative number.
What were my numbers?

$$\boxed{+} - \boxed{+} - \boxed{-} = 3$$

My answer was 3.
I started at −50.
Which 2 negative numbers did I subtract?

$$\boxed{-50} - \boxed{-} - \boxed{-} = 3$$

My answer was 3
I started at −50.
Which 3 negative numbers did I subtract?

$$\boxed{-50} - \boxed{-} - \boxed{-} - \boxed{-} = 3$$

Add-on
What would happen if the answer was changed to 2 or 4?
What can you say about the solutions?

Number wheel 1

Put the numbers in the wheel so that the 3 numbers in a line total 128.
One has been done for you.

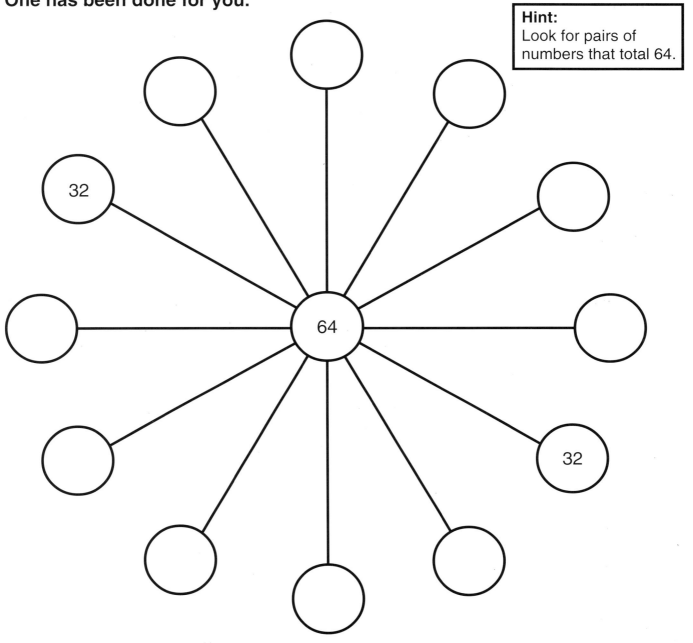

Hint:
Look for pairs of
numbers that total 64.

~~32~~	29	47
35	17	~~32~~
21	19	43
45	51	13

How to Dazzle at Written Calculations

Number wheel 2

Put the numbers in the wheel so that the 3 numbers in a line total 1.
One has been done for you.

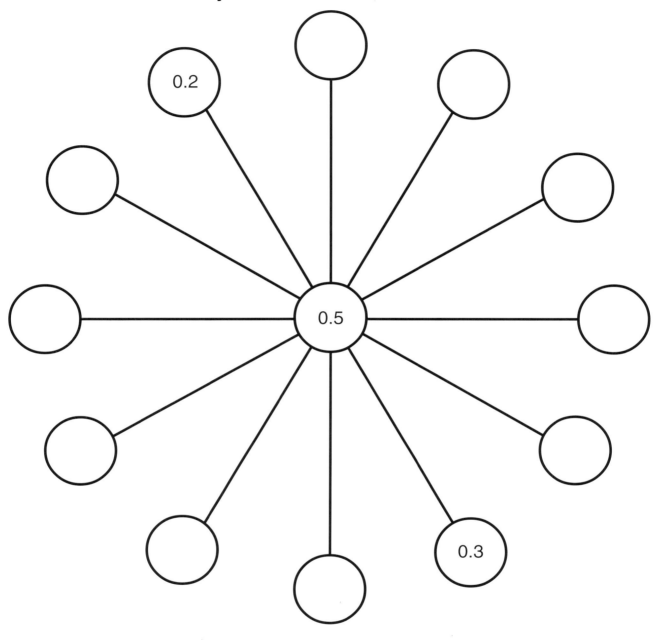

0.2	0.1	0.25
0.15	0.01	0.05
0.4	0.25	0.3
0.49	0.45	0.35

Number wheel 3

Put the fractions in the wheel so that the 3 numbers in a line total 1.
One has been done for you.

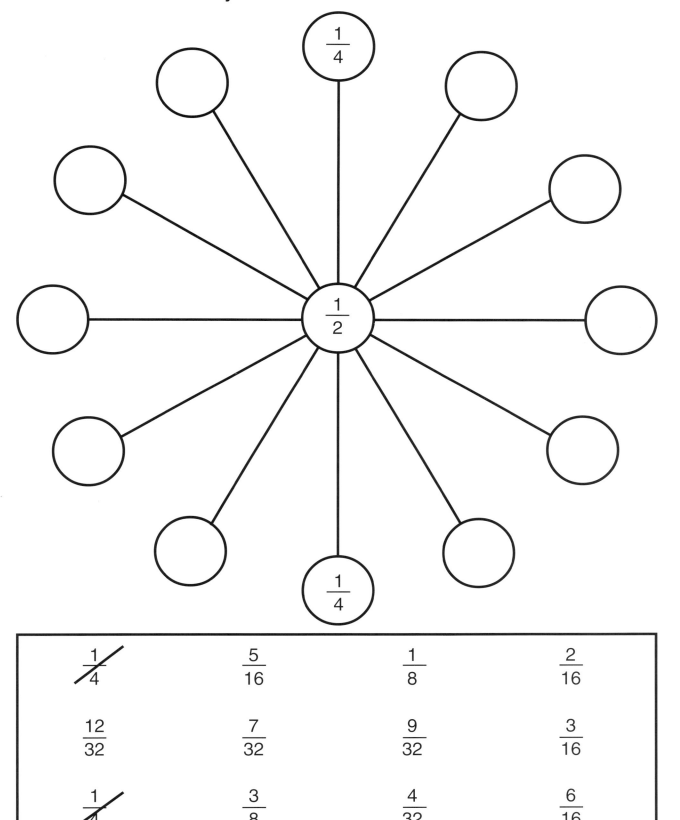

$\frac{1}{4}$	$\frac{5}{16}$	$\frac{1}{8}$	$\frac{2}{16}$
$\frac{12}{32}$	$\frac{7}{32}$	$\frac{9}{32}$	$\frac{3}{16}$
$\frac{1}{4}$	$\frac{3}{8}$	$\frac{4}{32}$	$\frac{6}{16}$

How to Dazzle at Written Calculations

Find the cost of one

Example

. 6 cartons of milk cost £1.98. How much do 9 cartons cost?

1 carton   £1.98 ÷ 6 = £0.33 (33p)

9 cartons   £0.33 x 9 = £2.97

4 pencils cost £1.	6 pencils cost?
2 CDs cost £13.98.	5 CDs cost?
3 magazines cost £7.50.	2 magazines cost?
4 T-shirts cost £39.96.	3 T-shirts cost?
5 cans of cola cost £2.	3 cans of cola cost?
4 rubbers cost £1.20.	How many rubbers for £1.80?
2 pens for 98p.	How many pens for £9.80?
Hot dogs cost £1.50 for 2.	How many can I buy for £10? Do I have any change?

Add-on
Choose 3 items from above. How much do they cost altogether?
Which 3 items would cost least? Which 3 items would cost most?

Supporters' shop

The football club's supporters' shop sells:

Scarves

Shirts

£1.50

Badges

One scarf and one badge costs £11.50.

Two shirts and one scarf costs £40.

Three badges and two shirts costs £34.50.

How much does each item cost?

Scarves	Shirts	Badges

How much for:

- two scarves?

- three shirts?

- four badges?

How much altogether?

CDs

Andrew wanted six new CDs.

A £ _____

B £ _____

C £ _____

D £ _____

E £ _____

F £ _____

Hint:
Round the prices to
whole pounds.

A and D would cost £11.98.

D and F would cost £17.98.

F and B would cost £16.98.

B and C would cost £21.98.

C and E would cost £18.98.

How much does each CD cost? Write the prices under the CDs.

Add-on
How much would they cost altogether?

Internal and external angles

Types of angles:
A right angle is 90°.

Internal angles are the angles inside the shape.

A triangle has 3 internal angles. All the angles inside a triangle add up to 180°.

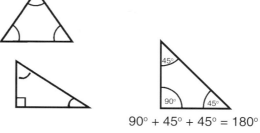

$$90° + 45° + 45° = 180°$$

External angles are the angles outside the shape. Each of these angles and the internal angles add up to 360°.

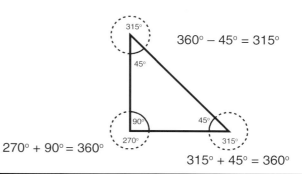

$$360° - 45° = 315°$$

$$270° + 90° = 360°$$

$$315° + 45° = 360°$$

What are the external angles?

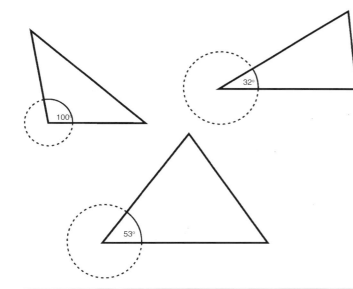

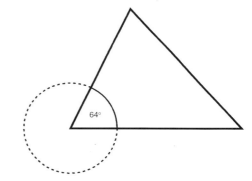

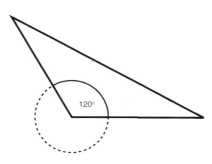

Add-on
What are the internal angles?

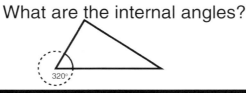

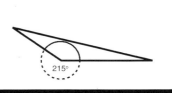

How to Dazzle at Written Calculations

Half price sale

Everything is half price! Work out the sale prices. Think carefully about what price you put for items costing odd amounts.

£35   sale price

£199   sale price

FRIZZ in concert
£15   sale price

£39   sale price

£59.99   sale price

TERROR OF THE DEEP
£12.75   sale price

£10.99   sale price

£65.75   sale price

Add-on
What price would you put if a further 20% was taken off the sale price?

Using factors

You can make multiplication easier if you split one of the numbers into its factors.

For example:	43 x 14 [7 x 2 = 14]
	43 x 7 = 301
	301 x 2 = 602
so	43 x 14 = 602 (43 x 7 x 2)

Try these:

Multiplication	Factors	Interim stage	Solution
19 x 16	4 x 4 = 16	19 x 4 = 76	76 x 4 = 304
32 x 24	6 x 4 = 24	32 x 6 = 192	192 x 4 =
21 x 49	7 x 7 = 49	21 x 7 =	
94 x 45	9 x 5 =		
107 x 15			
394 x 36			
76 x 72			
81 x 18			
38 x 63			

How to Dazzle at Written Calculations

Grid multiplication 1

35 x 6

Hint: 35 = 30 + 5

x	30	5
6	180	30

35 x 6 = 180 + 30 = 210

---

23 x 4

x	20	3
4		

23 x 4 = ☐ ☐ ☐

---

47 x 3

x	40	7

47 x 3 = ☐ + ☐ = ☐

---

61 x 7

x		

61 x 7 = ☐ + ☐ = ☐

---

59 x 5

x		

☐ x ☐ = ☐ + ☐ = ☐

Add-on

Try these for yourself:

16 x 9 87 x 8 32 x 6

Grid multiplication 2

437 x 4

x	400	30	7
4	1600	120	28

437 x 4 = 1600 + 120 + 28 = 1748

---

316 x 5

x	300	10	6
5			

316 x 5 = ☐ + ☐ + ☐ = ☐

---

582 x 3

x	500	80	2

582 x 3 = ☐ + ☐ + ☐ = ☐

---

764 x 8

x			

764 x 8 = ☐ + ☐ + ☐ = ☐

---

943 x 6

x			

943 x 6 = ☐ + ☐ + ☐ = ☐

Add-on

Try these for yourself:

627 x 3   876 x 7   943 x 5

Grid multiplication 3

37 x 24

x	30	7	
20	600	140	740
4	120	28	148

Hint: 37 = 30 + 7
24 = 20 + 4

37 x 24 = 740 + 148 = 888

42 x 31

x	40	2	
30			
1			

42 x 31 = ☐ + ☐ = ☐

57 x 19

x	50	7	
10			
9			

57 x 19 = ☐ + ☐ = ☐

63 x 27

x	60	3	

63 x 27 = ☐ + ☐ = ☐

79 x 53

x		

79 x 53 = ☐ + ☐ = ☐

86 x 39

x		

86 x 39 = ☐ + ☐ = ☐

Add-on
Try these for yourself:
62 x 13   94 x 76   59 x 32

Grid multiplication 4

423 x 37

x	400	20	3	
30	12000	600	90	12690
7	2800	140	21	2961

Hint: 423 = 400 + 20 + 3
37 = 30 + 7

423 x 37 = 12690 + 2961 = 15651

---

274 x 23

x	200	70	4	
20				
3				

274 x 23 = ☐ + ☐ = ☐

---

319 x 16

x	300	10	9	

319 x 16 = ☐ + ☐ = ☐

---

547 x 49

x	500	40	7	

547 x 49 = ☐ + ☐ = ☐

---

716 x 25

x		

716 x 25 = ☐ + ☐ = ☐

---

851 x 26

x		

851 x 26 = ☐ + ☐ = ☐

Add-on
Think about how you could work out:

423 x 3.7   274 x 2.3   319 x 1.6   54.7 x 49   71.6 x 25   85.1 x 2.6

How to Dazzle at Written Calculations

Grid multiplication 5

3 x 1.9

x	1	0.9
3	3	2.7

Hint: 1.9 = 1 + 0.9

$3 \times 1.9 = 3 + 2.7 = 5.7$

---

7 x 2.4

x	2	0.4
7		

$7 \times 2.4 = \boxed{} + \boxed{} = \boxed{}$

---

6 x 5.2

x	5	0.2

$6 \times 5.2 = \boxed{} + \boxed{} = \boxed{}$

---

9 x 3.6

x	3	0.6

$9 \times 3.6 = \boxed{} + \boxed{} = \boxed{}$

---

8 x 4.9

x		

$8 \times 4.9 = \boxed{} + \boxed{} = \boxed{}$

---

4 x 1.8

x		

$4 \times 1.8 = \boxed{} + \boxed{} = \boxed{}$

Add-on

Think about how you could work out:

0.3 x 1.9   0.7 x 2.4   0.6 x 5.2   0.9 x 3.6   0.8 x 4.9   0.4 x 1.8

Grid multiplication 6

2.4 x 1.7

x	1	0.7	
2	2	1.4	3.4
0.4	0.4	0.28	0.68

Hint: 2.4 = 2 + 0.4
1.7 = 1 + 0.7

2.4 x 1.7 = 3.4 + 0.68 = 4.08

3.9 x 2.4

x	2	0.4	
3			
0.9			

3.9 x 2.4 = ☐ + ☐ = ☐

5.2 x 6.8

x	6	0.8	

5.2 x 6.8 = ☐ + ☐ = ☐

7.3 x 4.8

x			

7.3 x 4.8 = ☐ + ☐ = ☐

6.9 x 3.2

x			

6.9 x 3.2 = ☐ + ☐ = ☐

7.4 x 8.9

x			

7.4 x 8.9 = ☐ + ☐ = ☐

Add-on

Think about how you could work out:

2.4 x 0.17   3.9 x 0.24   0.52 x 6.8   0.73 x 4.8   0.69 x 0.32   0.74 x 0.89

Stacking 1

35 x 6

x	30	5
6	180	30

35 x 6 = 180 + 30 = 210

Grid method

```
    35
  x  6
  ─────
    30    6 x 5
   180    6 x 30
  ─────
   210    6 x 35
```

Stacking method

---

24 x 7

```
    24
  x  7
  ─────

  ─────
```

63 x 4

```
    63
  x  4
  ─────

  ─────
```

46 x 9

```
    46
  x  9
  ─────

  ─────
```

58 x 6

```
    58
  x  6
  ─────

  ─────
```

Add-on

Think about the answers to:
350 x 6
240 x 7
63 x 40
46 x 90
580 x 60

Stacking 2

469 x 5			742 x 3	
	469			742
	x 5			x 3
	———			———
	45	5 x 9		
	300	5 x 60		
	2000	5 x 400		
	———			———
	2345			

316 x 6			856 x 4	
	316			
	x 6			x
	———			———
		6 x 6		
		6 x 10		
		6 x 300		
	———			———

647 x 8		964 x 9	
	x		x
	———		———
	———		———

Add-on
Think about the answers to:

46.9 x 5	31.6 x 6	647 x 0.8
7.42 x 3	8.56 x 4	9.64 x 0.9

Standard method – multiplication 1

469 x 5		**1**	**2**	**3**
		4 6 9	4 6 9	4 6 9
		x 5	x 5	x 5
		5	4 5	2 3 4 5
		4	3 4	3 4

347 x 3	3 4 7 x 3	624 x 5	6 2 4 x 5
762 x 7	x	894 x 2	x
949 x 6	x	302 x 4	x
609 x 3	x		

Add-on
Think about the answers to:

469 x 50	347 x 30	762 x 70	94.9 x 6
60.9 x 3	624 x 50	89.4 x 2	30.2 x 4

Standard method – multiplication 2

429 x 36		
	4 2 9	
	x 3 6	
	2 5 7 4	6 x 429
	1 2 8 7 0	30 x 429
	1 5 4 4 4	
	1 1	

Hint:
429 x 36 is approximately
400 x 40 = 16000

Always try an approximation first.

376 x 24

Approximation
400 x 20
= [   ]

    3 7 6
x   2 4
_____   4 x 376
             20 x 376
_____

532 x 41

Approximation
500 x 40
= [   ]

    5 3 2
x   4 1
_____   1 x 532
             40 x 532
_____

675 x 27

Approximation
700 x [   ]
= [   ]

    6 7 5
x   2 7
_____
_____

Add-on
Think about the
answers to
429 x 3.6
376 x 2.4
5.32 x 41
67.5 x 27
8.14 x 3.4

814 x 34

Approximation
[   ] x [   ]
= [   ]

    8 1 4
x   3 4
_____
_____

Standard method – multiplication 3

74.2 x 3

Approximation
75 x 3 = 225

```
  7 4 . 2
 x     3
 2 2 2 . 6
      1
```

47.1 x 4

Approximation
50 x 4 = 200

```
  4 7 . 1
 x     4
```

39.2 x 6

Approximation

[ ] x [ ] = [ ]

```
  3 9 . 2
 x     6
```

6.42 x 4

Approximation

[ ] x [ ] = [ ]

```
 x
```

9.76 x 8

Approximation

[ ] x [ ] = [ ]

```
 x
```

6.04 x 3

Approximation

[ ] x [ ] = [ ]

```
 x
```

7.21 x 7

Approximation

[ ] x [ ] = [ ]

```
 x
```

1.04 x 3

Approximation

[ ] x [ ] = [ ]

```
 x
```

Add-on
Think about the answers to:
7.42 x 3
74.2 x 0.3
4.71 x 4
47.1 x 0.4
0.642 x 4
0.976 x 8

What's my multiplication?

My answer was 36.
Which 2 numbers did I multiply?

[   ] x [   ] = 36

My answer was 36.
Which 3 numbers did I multiply?

[   ] x [   ] x [   ] = 36

My answer was 36.
Which 4 numbers did I multiply?

[   ] x [   ] x [   ] x [   ] = 36

My answer was 36.
Which 2 negative numbers did I multiply?

[–] x [–] = 36

My answer was 36.
Which 2 negative numbers and 1 positive number did I multiply?

[–] x [–] x [   ] = 36

My answer was 36.
Which 2 negative numbers and 2 positive numbers did I multiply?

[–] x [–] x [   ] x [   ] = 36

Add-on
Why can't you multiply 1 negative number and 1 positive number
to get 36 as the answer?

Sorting multiples

Venn diagrams are used to help sort information.

You can use a Venn diagram to sort multiples of 10 and 5 using numbers from 1 to 20:

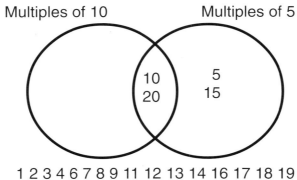

Multiples of 10   Multiples of 5

10
20   5
15

1 2 3 4 6 7 8 9 11 12 13 14 16 17 18 19

What can you say about the numbers that are outside the Venn diagram?

_____

Why are 10 and 20 in both circles?_____

Try these using numbers from 1 to 30.

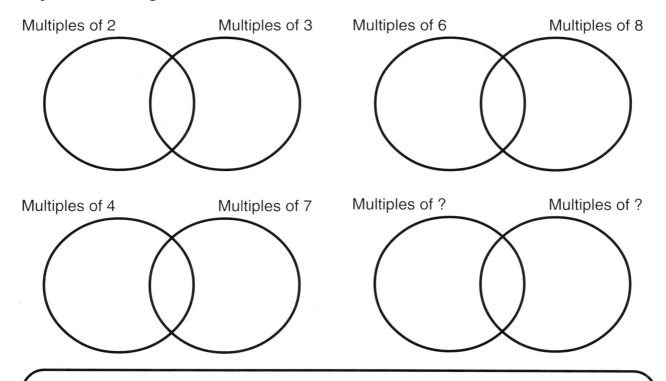

Multiples of 2   Multiples of 3   Multiples of 6   Multiples of 8

Multiples of 4   Multiples of 7   Multiples of ?   Multiples of ?

Add-on
Make some statements about what you have noticed.

Increasing the proportions

Here is the start of a recipe for 3 people.

Cheese and Potato Bake
300g grated cheese
600g sliced cooked potatoes
30g butter
pinch of salt and pepper

Now work out the ingredients for 4 people.

What amount of cheese would you buy for 9 people?

How do you increase the amount of salt and pepper?

Add-on
Think about how you could work out the ingredients for 5 people.

Multiplication and division words

**Look at these words. Check you know what they mean.
Sort them into two groups.**

times	twice	division
share	divide	halve
remainder	**quotient**	multiply
multiplication	lots of	**product**
dividend	**divisible**	groups of

X

÷

Add-on
Make up sentences using the words in **bold**.

Division shapes 1

Put the same number at each corner of the shapes.

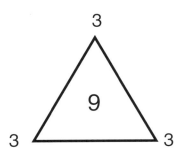

108

2528

585

1974

7568

Division shapes 2

Put the same number at each corner of the shapes.

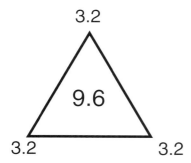

25.6

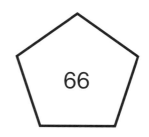

568.2

325.6

136.76

125.1

367.2

40.32

Add-on
Make up a puzzle using a nonagon.

Chunking 1

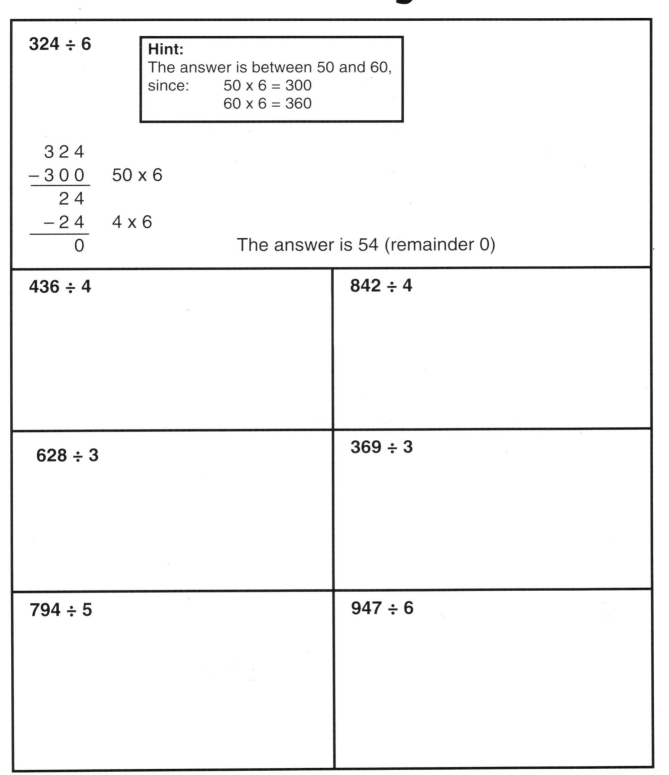

324 ÷ 6

Hint:
The answer is between 50 and 60,
since: 50 x 6 = 300
             60 x 6 = 360

```
    3 2 4
  − 3 0 0      50 x 6
    ───────
      2 4
    − 2 4      4 x 6
    ───────
        0
```
The answer is 54 (remainder 0)

436 ÷ 4	**842 ÷ 4**
628 ÷ 3	**369 ÷ 3**
794 ÷ 5	**947 ÷ 6**

Add-on

Use a calculator to check your answers. First multiply your answer
by the divisor and then add on the remainder. You should get the
number you started with.

Chunking 2

216 ÷ 14

> **Hint:**
> The answer is between 10 and 20,
> since: 10 x 14 = 140
>   20 x 14 = 280

```
   2 1 6
 − 1 4 0     10 x 14
     7 6
   − 7 0     5 x 14
       6
```

The answer is 15 (remainder 6)

394 ÷ 17	**427 ÷ 21**
642 ÷ 33	**946 ÷ 27**
854 ÷ 36	**726 ÷ 48**

Add-on

Use a calculator to check your answers. First multiply the answer by the divisor then add on the remainder. You should get the number you started with.

What's my division?

My answer was 7.
Which 2 numbers did I use to divide?

$$\boxed{} \div \boxed{} = 7$$

My answer was 7 remainder 1.
Which 2 numbers did I use to divide?

$$\boxed{} \div \boxed{} = 7 \text{ remainder } 1$$

My answer was 7 remainder 1.
I started with 43.
What did I divide with?

$$\boxed{43} \div \boxed{} = 7 \text{ remainder } 1$$

My answer was 7 remainder 2.
Which two numbers did I use to divide?

$$\boxed{} \div \boxed{} = 7 \text{ remainder } 2$$

Try for   7 remainder 3

                7 remainder 4

                7 remainder 5

                7 remainder 6

What is the relationship with the 7 times table?

Add-on
What happens if you use negative numbers?

Division problems

6 eggs are packed in a box. How many boxes would you need for 342 eggs?

_____

Each CD costs £12. How many would cost £288?

_____

There are 750 students in the school. There are 25 students per class. How many classes of 25 are there?

_____

217 students are going on a trip to Chessington World of Adventures. The school hires coaches which hold 48 students. How many coaches do they need?

_____

A meal for 4 friends in a burger bar costs £15.20 in total. They each have the same. How much should they each pay?

_____

The journey to and from school is 190 miles per month. How long is each one-way journey? (Assume there are 20 school days in a month.)

_____

Add-on
Discuss how you can tell if a number is divisible by 2, 3, 5 and 10.

Holiday costings

A family of four people – two adults and two children want to go on holiday to Florida for two weeks.

✳   The cost for an adult is £699 and for a child is £507.
     How much would it cost altogether?

_____

✳   A sea view costs £4 extra per person per night.
     How much extra would this be?

_____

✳   The supplement for a day flight is £20 per person.
     How much extra would this be?

_____

✳   A hire car costs £149 for the first five days and £25 per day after
     that. How much would a hire car cost for two weeks?

_____

✳   The hotel charges £10 for breakfast for an adult and £7 for a child.
     How much would breakfast cost the family per day? How much for
     the two weeks?

_____

✳   How much would the two-week holiday in Florida with a sea view,
     day flights, a hire car for the fortnight and breakfast on each day
     cost the family?

_____

Add-on
Look in a holiday brochure and find the cost of a holiday
in Spain for the family.

Family day trip

A family of two adults and two children went to Brighton for the day.

* They spent £54 on train tickets. The children travelled at half price. How much were the adult tickets?

   _____

* They spent £50 in a restaurant for lunch. How much was that each on average?

   _____

* They bought a T-shirt each and an ice-cream for each of the children. It cost £42.50. How much were the T-shirts?

   _____

Ice-cream £1.25 each

* They took a taxi back to the station. It went 4.2 miles and cost £13.02. How much was that per mile?

   _____

* How much did the whole day cost them? _____

* How much is this per person on average? _____

Add-on
How much extra would it have cost if both children had taken a friend with them who bought the same things?

Is it close enough?

There are times when it is necessary to calculate exactly, times when it is OK to approximate and other times when it is important to over estimate.

Discuss with a friend whether it is OK to use approximations in each of these circumstances.

A gardener working out how much fertiliser to put on her lawn.

A teacher working out test results.

A pilot plotting a course over the Atlantic Ocean.

An engineer designing a footbridge over a canal.

A car designer drawing a prototype car.

A shopkeeper checking a day's takings.

A group of young people ordering drinks in a café.

A doctor prescribing medicine.

A teenager working out how much paint to buy to decorate his bedroom.

Add-on
Think of 3 new scenarios when accuracy would matter.

It's close enough!

You don't always have to work out calculations exactly. Sometimes an approximation will do.

For instance, if you wanted to know if you had enough money to pay for two CDs – one costing £6.99 and the other costing £11.99 – it would be OK to round the amounts to £7 and £12.

Work out an approximate total for each shopping expedition.

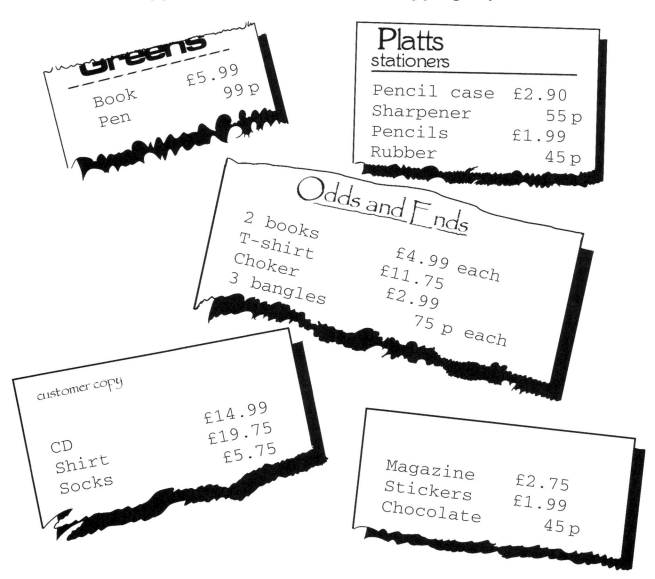

Greens
Book	£5.99
Pen	99 p

Platts stationers
Pencil case	£2.90
Sharpener	55 p
Pencils	£1.99
Rubber	45 p

Odds and Ends
2 books	£4.99 each
T-shirt	£11.75
Choker	£2.99
3 bangles	75 p each

customer copy
CD	£14.99
Shirt	£19.75
Socks	£5.75

Magazine	£2.75
Stickers	£1.99
Chocolate	45 p

Add-on
Choose an outfit of clothes from a catalogue.
Work out an approximate cost.

Products

You will need a copy of the product square (page 48).

Write any products from the product square in the grid below.
Work as a team. Fill up the grid.

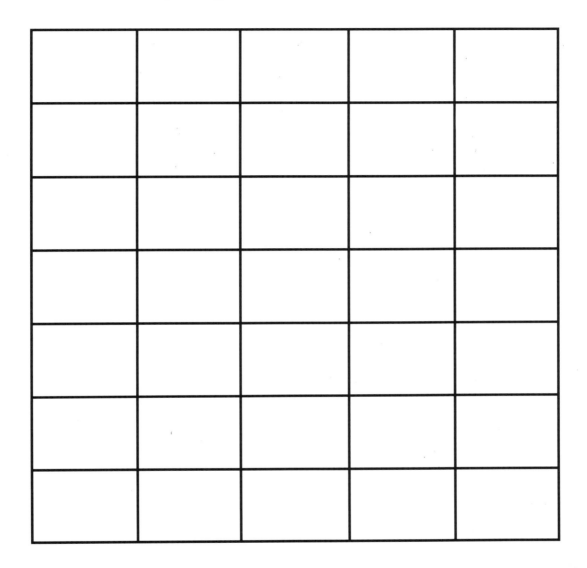

Choose pairs of numbers from a pack of 1 to 10 number cards and cross out the 'product' on your grid if it is there. The first team to get four in a row is the winner.

Add-on
Work out some products that would give you a better chance of winning.
Play the game again.

Areas of rectangles

These are the areas of some rectangles.

What are the possible lengths and widths of each of the rectangles?

Length	Width	Area
		24cm^2
		36cm^2
		63cm^2
		180mm^2
		540mm^2
		960mm^2
		50m^2
		42m^2

Add-on
Find five different possible lengths and widths of a rectangle with an area of 3600mm^2.

Areas of squares

These are the areas of some squares.

What lengths are the sides?

Side	Area
	25cm²
	64cm²
	160mm²
	490mm²
	9m²
	81m²
	100cm²
	1681mm²

Add-on
Use your product square to help you make up some more.
Work them out in mm².

Check test 1

1.	9 more than 197	
2.	19 less than 217	
3.	A pair of shoes cost £22.00. The price was increased by 10% after the sale. How much do they cost now?	
4.	A pair of shoes cost £25.00. The price was reduced by 10% in the sale. How much do they cost now?	
5.	What is the difference between 54 and 81?	
6.	What is the sum of these three numbers? 129, 347, 531	
7.	573 minus 482	
8.	−7 add −8 add −5	
9.	−3 + −7 + 4 =	
10.	0.15 plus 0.25 plus 0.3	

Check test 2

1.	A third add a sixth	
2.	The area of a square is 49 centimetres squared. What lengths are the sides?	
3.	73 multiplied by 6	
4.	Three hundred and eighty-five times three	
5.	Eight hundred and sixty-five divided by five	
6.	8 cakes are packed in a box. How many boxes would you need for 432 cakes?	
7.	What is the product of 6 and 8?	
8.	What are the factors for 28?	
9.	A car costs £59.50 to hire for one day. How much will it cost for three days?	
10.	What is the remainder when you divide 77 by 9?	

Product square

x	1	2	3	4	5	6	7	8	9	10
1	1	2	3	4	5	6	7	8	9	10
2	2	4	6	8	10	12	14	16	18	20
3	3	6	9	12	15	18	21	24	27	30
4	4	8	12	16	20	24	28	32	36	40
5	5	10	15	20	25	30	35	40	45	50
6	6	12	18	24	30	36	42	48	54	60
7	7	14	21	28	35	42	49	56	63	70
8	8	16	24	32	40	48	56	64	72	80
9	9	18	27	36	45	54	63	72	81	90
10	10	20	30	40	50	60	70	80	90	100